The Official
ASTON VILLA
FOOTBALL CLUB ANNUAL
2017

Compiled by Rob Bishop and Tricia Mills

A Grange Publication

© 2016. Published by Grange Communications Ltd., Edinburgh, under licence from Aston Villa Football Club. Printed in the EU.

Every effort has been made to ensure the accuracy of information within this publication but the publishers cannot be held responsible for any errors or omissions. Views expressed are those of the author and do not necessarily represent those of the publishers or the football club. All rights reserved.

Special thanks to Gayner Monkton

Photographs ©Neville Williams and Getty Images

ISBN 978-1-911287-01-8

Club Honours

EUROPEAN CUP
WINNERS: 1981-82
QUARTER-FINALISTS: 1982-83

EUROPEAN SUPER CUP
WINNERS: 1982-83

WORLD CLUBS CHAMPIONSHIP
RUNNERS-UP: 1982

INTERTOTO CUP
WINNERS: 2001

FOOTBALL LEAGUE
CHAMPIONS: 1893-94, 1895-96, 1896-97, 1898-99,
1899-1900, 1909-10, 1980-81
RUNNERS-UP: 1888-89, 1902-03, 1907-08, 1910-11,
1912-13, 1913-14, 1930-31, 1932-33, 1989-90

PREMIER LEAGUE
RUNNERS-UP: 1992-93

DIVISION TWO
CHAMPIONS: 1937-38, 1959-60

DIVISION THREE
CHAMPIONS: 1971-72

FA CUP
WINNERS: 1887, 1895, 1897, 1905, 1913, 1920, 1957
RUNNERS-UP: 1892, 1924, 2000, 2015

LEAGUE CUP
WINNERS: 1961, 1975, 1977, 1994, 1996
RUNNERS-UP: 1963, 1971, 2010

FA YOUTH CUP
WINNERS: 1972, 1980, 2002
RUNNERS-UP: 2004, 2010

NEXTGEN SERIES
WINNERS: 2013

Contents

THE NEW >> BOYS

Villa Park
That's my home!

Ross McCormack made an amazing revelation on the day he became the second most expensive player in the club's history – he had never been to Villa Park!

But the Scotland international soon familiarised himself with his new surroundings after his £12m transfer from Fulham, and he is determined to make our famous stadium a home from home over the next few seasons.

If the 30-year-old Scot's track record is any guide, he should contribute some crucial goals over the course of the next four seasons.

Having started his career in his home city with Glasgow Rangers, he has been a prolific marksman in the Championship for Cardiff City, Leeds United and Fulham over the past few years. Last season he netted 23 goals for the Cottagers, which is what prompted Roberto Di Matteo to sign him.

After signing his four-year contract, McCormack said: "This is a great club and it's very exciting to be part of this project to put the club back where it belongs, which is the Premier League."

Christmas comes early!

We all know what it's like to get excited ahead of a big event like Christmas or a holiday, and Albert Adomah is no different.

The hours were ticking down to the 11.00pm cut-off point when Albert's move from Middlesbrough was completed on transfer deadline day. And the attacking midfielder revealed he couldn't have been more thrilled to become a Villan.

"I was like a child," he admitted. "I couldn't sleep the night before – I was just like a big kid, looking forward to the next day."

Adomah's dream came true when he became the club's ninth signing of the summer transfer window which saw Villa eclipse even their 2015 haul of eight new players.

The London-born Ghan international signed a four-year contract and aims to emulate his form of last season, when he helped Boro to promotion to the Premier League.

The honeymoon is over!

Family should always come before football – but Tommy Elphick was willing to make an exception.

When the central defender learned that Villa were interested in signing him, he dashed back from his honeymoon to make sure his transfer from Bournemouth went smoothly.

"As soon as I heard about Villa's interest, it was something that turned my head," said the man who became Roberto Di Matteo's first signing for the club.

"I had five days of my honeymoon left, but my wife is very understanding in terms of football. It's what gives us our living and when a club like Villa come calling the least you can do is give up five days of your honeymoon."

Tommy began his professional career with his hometown club Brighton & Hove Albion, playing 182 games for the Seagulls and scoring nine goals.

He joined Bournemouth in 2012 and in his first season he was appointed captain as well as winning the local paper's player of the season award.

In four years at Dean Court, during which he played 142 games, he helped the Cherries climb from League One to the Premier League.

Manager Roberto Di Matteo said: "He knows what's required to win promotion to the Premier League from the Championship.

"That experience is invaluable."

Loving the Villa history...

History may not be everyone's favourite subject but we reckon Aaron Tshibola must have enjoyed it when he was at school.

The midfielder was certainly fascinated by Villa's illustrious history when he became Roberto Di Matteo's third summer signing.

"The history of this football club is there for all to see," he said. "It speaks for itself. I have been getting shivers reading through all the cups and titles this club has won. It's incredible.

"Aston Villa is a big club and everyone knows we should be in the Premier League. The club has been in a low point but I want to be part of that journey back up. It's a new era now, a fresh start."

Home, James!

It didn't take James Chester long to make himself at home in claret and blue.

Less than 48 hours after being signed from neighbours West Bromwich Albion, the central defender made his debut in Villa's first home game of the season.

He settled in immediately as Villa beat Rotherham United 3-0.

Chester knows what it takes to win promotion from the Championship, having helped Hull City to finish runners-up behind Cardiff City in 2013.

And it was Ross McCormack who helped him to achieve his dream.

Hull drew their final game 2-2 against Cardiff, but then had to wait while rivals Watford finished their match with Leeds, which had been delayed by 15 minutes.

It was 1-1 when Hull's game finished – but McCormack popped up with a late Leeds winner which meant the Tigers were up.

THE NEW >> BOYS

Aiming for a passion play!

Pierluigi Gollini intends to write his own love story with Villa after arriving from the city which provided the backdrop for one of the world's best-known plays.

The 21-year-old Italian keeper signed from the Hellas club in Verona, the setting of William Shakespeare's Romeo and Juliet. And while that particular tale had an unhappy end, Gollini is determined to enjoy every minute of his time at Villa Park.

"This is a very big opportunity," he said. "I am really happy to be here. The fans are very passionate and the stadium is magnificent."

The joke's on Ritchie...

Ritchie De Laet is always in positive mood – even when things are not going well on the pitch.

The Belgian defender, signed from Premier League champions Leicester City, said: "I like a joke and a prank, just to keep everyone going. If we have a bad result, you can't dwell on it, so I like to get smiles back on faces and get ready for the next game."

On the pitch, though, Ritchie is deadly serious, and last season he enjoyed double success. After playing for Leicester for the first few months he joined Middlesbrough on loan – and helped them to promotion.

We have lift-off...

Jonathan Kodjia got off to a flying start as a Villa player – without even kicking a ball. The ink was barely dry on the striker's contract before he flew off to join his Ivory Coast team-mates for an Africa Cup of Nations qualifying game against Sierra Leone.

But the former Bristol City star has his feet firmly on the ground when it comes to getting Villa back to English football's top flight.

"The Championship is very strong," he said. "Every game is hard because teams concentrate and run for 90 minutes.

"We need to be together, show solidarity and work hard. I want to play well for the club and I aim to score lots of goals." Jonathan certainly did that for Bristol City, hitting the target 20 times in 52 league and cup games for the Ashton Gate club. Born in the St. Denis area of Paris, he began his career with Reims. But it was during his season with Angers in 2014-15 that he really blossomed as a prolific marksman, scoring 15 goals as they won promotion to France's Ligue 1.

Blown away at Villa Park!

Mile Jedinak has played at most of English football's major venues during his time with Crystal Palace but Villa Park is the one which impressed him most.

"My first experience of this place was amazing," said the Australian defender, who watched Villa's early-season home match against Huddersfield Town and became a Villan a couple of days later.

"I have fond memories of playing at Villa Park. Everyone talks about the big stadiums and I've played at quite a few, but this was the one that really blew me away."

Alan **HUTTON**

Do you know

Ashley Westwood?

1 Ashley joined Villa on transfer deadline day in 2012. Can you remember which club he signed from?

  A. Chesterfield   B. Crewe Alexandra   C. Charlton Athletic

2 He made his Villa debut as a substitute on the day another new Villa signing also went on and scored the second goal in a 2-0 home win. Which team did we beat that day?

  A. Swansea City   B. Southampton   C. Sunderland

3 His first goal in claret-and-blue was a stunning 25-yard volley which earned a 2-2 draw after Villa had trailed 2-0 in an away game. Who were our opponents that night?

  A. West Brom   B. West Ham   C. Wigan Athletic

4 After going almost the whole of last season without scoring, Ashley netted twice in one game in April – against which team?

  A. Bournemouth   B. Southampton   C. Watford

5 Ashley is one of many Villa players whose names have been used as characters in the bestselling novels of which Villa-supporting author?

  A. John Grisham   B. Dan Brown   C. Lee Child

ANSWERS ON PAGE 60

No place like home!

The year 2017 marks the 120th anniversary of our home ground.

We have been proud to call Villa Park home since March 1897, when the club moved from Wellington Road in Perry Barr the week after winning a league and FA Cup double.

Since then, the stadium has undergone vast changes and hosted thousands of football matches plus various other events, including boxing, rugby and even rock concerts and religious gatherings.

As you can see from our photo of Villa Park in 1907, the current stadium bears no resemblance to its early days. The current North Stand was built in 1977, followed by the rebuilding of the Holte End (1994) the Doug Ellis Stand (1995) and the Trinity Road Stand (2001).

Celebrating 120 years at

10 fascinating facts and figures

We are celebrating 120 years of Villa Park in the Villa News & Record throughout this season. Here are 10 fascinating facts and figures with which to impress your friends:

- Villa Park has staged more FA Cup semi-finals – 55 – than any other venue.

- Floodlights were installed for the first time in 1958.

- The stadium's record attendance is 76,588 for an FA Cup quarter-final against Derby County in 1946.

- We have hosted England internationals across three centuries. The first was a 2-1 win over Scotland in 1899 and the last one was a 0-0 draw with Holland in 2005.

- Villa Park was a venue for three group games during the 1966 World Cup finals.

- We were hosts for four games at Euro 96, including the quarter-final between the Czech Republic and Portugal.

- We staged the last-ever UEFA Cup-Winners' Cup final in 1999, when Lazio of Italy beat Spain's Real Mallorca 2-1.

- The stadium was used for two games at the 2015 Rugby World Cup.

- The new Trinity Road Stand was opened by HRH Prince Charles – 77 years after his grandfather the Duke of York had officially opened the previous stand in 1924.

- Before its demolition, the Holte End was the largest behind-the-goal terrace in Europe. At one stage it held as many as 27,000 supporters.

Villa Park

Give us a clue!

Can you help Hercules identify these Villa players from the clues about them? Award yourself three points if you can answer after Clue A, two if you get it after Clue B and one if you need Clue C before naming the player in question. And why not test your knowledge against a Villa-supporting friend?

1
A. I WAS BORN IN BRIGHTON AND STARTED MY CAREER WITH MY HOMETOWN CLUB
B. I'M A CENTRAL DEFENDER
C. I JOINED VILLA FROM BOURNEMOUTH

2
A. I'M A MIDFIELDER WHO WAS BORN IN BIRMINGHAM
B. MY OLDER BROTHER USED TO PLAY FOR VILLA
C. I SPENT LAST SEASON ON LOAN TO NOTTINGHAM FOREST

3
A. I'M A STRIKER AND I WAS BORN IN FRANCE
B. I JOINED VILLA FROM BLACKBURN ROVERS
C. I SCORED ON MY DEBUT AT BOURNEMOUTH ON THE OPENING DAY OF LAST SEASON

4
A. I'M A MIDFIELDER AND I JOINED VILLA FOUR YEARS AGO
B. I MADE MY DEBUT AS A SUB AGAINST SWANSEA CITY, ALONG WITH CHRISTIAN BENTEKE
C. I PREVIOUSLY PLAYED FOR CREWE ALEXANDRA

5
A. I WAS BORN IN GLASGOW AND STARTED MY CAREER WITH A CLUB IN MY HOME CITY
B. I'M A STRIKER
C. I JOINED VILLA FROM FULHAM DURING THE SUMMER

6
A. I WAS BORN IN SCOTLAND AND I'M A DEFENDER
B. I JOINED VILLA FROM TOTTENHAM HOTSPUR IN AUGUST 2011
C. WHEN I SIGNED, I WAS INTERVIEWED BY AVTV – UNDER THE FLOODLIGHTS AT VILLA PARK!

ANSWERS ON PAGE 61

International Villans

VILLA HAVE HAD MANY OVERSEAS PLAYERS DOWN THE YEARS. CAN YOU IDENTIFY 12 OF THEM – ALL FROM DIFFERENT COUNTRIES – WITH THE HELP OF JACK GREALISH'S NAME?

TO HELP YOU, WE HAVE REVEALED THE PLAYERS' NATIONALITIES, POSITIONS AND THE YEARS THEY SIGNED FOR VILLA.

1. Moustapha H - Moroccan who joined us from Coventry City in 2001.

2. Milan B - Czech Republic striker signed from Liverpool in 2005.

3. Ulises D - Ecuadorian full-back signed from Hibernian in 2002.

4. Dwight Y - Trinidad & Tobago striker who arrived in 1989.

5. Juan Pablo A - Colombian striker signed from River Plate of Argentina in 2001.

6. Stiliyan P - Bulgarian midfielder who joined from Celtic in 2006.

7. Savo M - Serbian striker signed from Partizan Belgrade in 1995.

8. Aplay O - Turkish defender who joined from Fenerbahce in 2000.

9. David G - French winger signed from Tottenham in 2000.

10. Carles G - Spanish midfielder who arrived from Valencia in 2015.

11. Stefan P - Dutch keeper who signed from De Graafschap in 2002.

12. Ronny J - Norwegian defender snapped up on a free transfer from Man United in 2002.

Crossword column letters: J A C K G R E A L I S H

ANSWERS ON PAGE 61

MEET THE BOSS

Roberto Di Matteo became Villa's 27th manager when he was appointed in June. Here are a few facts and figures about the new boss...

On a Swiss roll...

Although he had Italian parents, Roberto was actually born in Switzerland, at a place called Schaffhausen, on 29th May 1970.

He started his football career with his hometown club in 1988, and also played for two other Swiss clubs, Zurich and Aarau.

In 1993, he helped Aarau to the Swiss title, and was also voted Switzerland's Player of the Year.

When in Rome

In 1993 he moved to Rome to join Lazio, who were managed at the time by Italian goalkeeping legend Dino Zoff.

Although he signed for Lazio on a free transfer, he quickly established himself, making 87 Serie A appearances and scoring seven goals.

During his time at Lazio, he also broke into the Italy team, making his international debut against Croatia in November 1994. He went on to win 34 caps and score two goals for the national side, representing his country at both Euro 96 in England and the 1998 World Cup finals in France.

A record signing

It may not seem a vast amount in today's transfer market, but when Di Matteo joined Chelsea in 1996, his fee of £4.9m was a record for the Stamford Bridge club.

He was signed by Ruud Gullit, and despite suffering a broken leg early in the 2000-01 season, he went on to play a total of 175 league and cup games for Chelsea, scoring 26 goals.

Wembley woe - and joy

Roberto is the 18th Villa manager to have played against us – and he inflicted one of the most painful blows in the club's history at Wembley in 2000.

The last FA Cup final to be played beneath the stadium's famous twin towers – Chelsea v Villa – was settled in the 72nd-minute when Di Matteo poked the ball home from close range after Villa keeper David James had been unable to hold a free-kick from Gianfranco Zola.

It was the third time he had scored

in a Wembley final. In 1997 he scored after just 42 seconds – then the fastest goal in a Wembley FA Cup final – as Chelsea beat Middlesbrough. And he was also on target against Boro in the League Cup final the following year.

No wonder he was disappointed when the old stadium was demolished!

Dons Di Matteo

Roberto began his managerial career with Milton Keynes Dons in 2008, leading them to third place in League One, and the following season he steered our neighbours West Bromwich Albion to promotion from the Championship.

But it was at Chelsea that he made his biggest impact, leading them both to FA Cup and UEFA Champions League glory in 2012. The Blues beat Liverpool in the FA Cup final and Bayern Munich on penalties in the Champions League final – which was played at the German club's Allianz Arena.

His most recent job before joining Villa was manager of another German club, Schalke 04.

WHAT YEAR DID

You may need a little help from an older Villa fan, but see if you can identify the years in which these significant claret-and-blue events took place.

2. Villa are under pressure against West Brom in an FA Cup semi-final replay at St Andrew's. But a Billy Myerscough goal secured a place in the final.
(a) 1957   (b) 1958   (c) 1959

1. One team, two trophies. Villa's players parade the FA Cup and the League Championship trophy after winning the double.
(a) 1895   (b) 1896   (c) 1897

3. Third Division Villa put Tottenham Hotspur under pressure during the League Cup final at Wembley. Spurs won 2-0 with two late goals.
(a) 1970   (b) 1971   (c) 1972

4. Gordon Smith, skipper Chris Nicholl and two-goal Brian Little celebrate after a dramatic 3-2 League Cup triumph over Everton at Old Trafford.
(a) 1976   (b) 1977   (c) 1978

IT HAPPEN?

Answers on page 61

5. Dennis Mortimer, manager Tony Barton and match-winner Peter Withe show off the European Cup to Villa fans in Rotterdam.
(a) 1982   (b) 1983   (c) 1984

6. We're going up! Garry Thompson and the Villa faithful celebrate promotion from the Second Division after a goalless draw at Swindon.
(a) 1986   (b) 1987   (c) 1988

7. Dalian Atkinson heads a late goal to take the second leg of the League Cup semi-final against Tranmere Rovers to extra-time. Villa eventually win on penalties.
(a) 1992   (b) 1993   (c) 1994

8. On the ball – Villa midfielder Peter Whittingham is in happy mood after scoring the first goal with the Premier League's new high-visibility ball.
(a) 2003   (b) 2004   (c) 2005

9. John Carew heads one of his two goals in a 5-1 derby demolition of Birmingham City at Villa Park.
(a) 2008   (b) 2009   (c) 2010

10. Gabby Agbonlahor throws his shirt to Villa fans after scoring in a 2-2 draw against Everton at Goodison Park.
(a) 2010   (b) 2011   (c) 2012

PLAYER FILES

Jed
Steer

Born	NORWICH, 23.09.92
Signed	JULY 2013
Previous club	NORWICH CITY
Debut	ROTHERHAM UNITED (H) 28.08.13

Alan
Hutton

Born	GLASGOW, 30.11.84
Signed	AUGUST 2011
Previous club	TOTTENHAM HOTSPUR
Debut	EVERTON (A) 10.09.11

Aly
Cissokho

Born	BLOIS, FRANCE, 15.09.87
Signed	AUGUST 2014
Previous club	VALENCIA
Debut	STOKE CITY (A) 16.08.14

DEFENDER

Ritchie
De Laet

Born	ANTWERP, BELGIUM, 28.11.88
Signed	AUGUST 2016
Previous club	LEICESTER CITY
Debut	BRISTOL CITY (A) 27.08.16

GOALKEEPER

Pierluigi
Gollini

Born	BOLOGNA, ITALY, 18 .03.95
Signed	JULY 2016
Previous club	HELLAS VERONA
Debut	SHEFFIELD WEDNESDAY (A) 07.08.16

MIDFIELDER

Jordan
Lyden

Born	PERTH, AUSTRALIA, 30.01.96
Signed	ACADEMY GRADUATE
Debut	WYCOMBE WANDERERS (A) 09.01.2016

CENTRE-BACK

James
Chester

Born	WARRINGTON, 23.01.89
Signed	AUGUST 2016
Previous Club	WEST BROMWICH ALBION
Debut	ROTHERHAM UNITED (H) 13.08.16

CENTRE-BACK

Nathan
Baker

Born	WORCESTER, 23.04.91
Signed	ACADEMY GRADUATE
Debut	WIGAN ATHLETIC (A) 21.01.11

MIDFIELDER

Gary
Gardner

Born	SOLIHUILL, 26.02.92
Signed	ACADEMY GRADUATE
Debut	CHELSEA (A) 31.12.11

MIDFIELDER

Leandro
Bacuna

Born	GRONINGEN, HOLLAND 21.08.91
Signed	JUNE 2013
Previous club	GRONINGEN
Debut	ARSENAL (A) 18.08.2013

MIDFIELDER

Ashley
Westwood

Born	NANTWICH, 01.04.90
Signed	AUGUST 2012
Previous club	CREWE ALEXANDRA
Debut	SWANSEA CITY (H) 15.09.12

Jonathan
Kodjia

Born	PARIS, 22.10.89
Signed	AUGUST 2016
Previous club	BRISTOL CITY

Tommy
Elphick

Born	BRIGHTON, 07.09.87
Signed	JUNE 2016
Previous club	BOURNEMOUTH
Debut	SHEFFIELD WEDNESDAY (A) 07.08.16

Gabby
Agbonlahor

Born	BIRMINGHAM, 13.10.86
Signed	ACADEMY GRADUATE
Debut	EVERTON (A) 18.03.06

Micah
Richards

Born	BIRMINGHAM, 24.06.88
Signed	JUNE 2015
Previous club	MANCHESTER CITY
Debut	BOURNEMOUTH (A) 08.08.15

Libor
Kozak

Born	OPAVA, CZECH REPUBLIC, 30.05.89
Signed	SEPTEMBER 2013
Previous club	LAZIO
Debut	NEWCASTLE UNITED (H) 14.09.13

Jack
Grealish

Born	BIRMINGHAM, 10.09.95
Signed	ACADEMY GRADUATE
Debut	MANCHESTER CITY (A) 07.05.14

Kevin
Toner

Born	DUBLIN 18 .06.96
Signed	ACADEMY GRADUATE
Debut	SOUTHAMPTON (H) 23.04.16

Aaron
Tshibola

Born	NEWHAM, LONDON 02.01.9
Signed	JULY 2016
Previous club	READING
Debut	SHEFFIELD WEDNESDAY (A) 07.08.16

MIDFIELDER

(On Loan)

Carlos Sanchez

Born	QUIBDO, COLOMBIA 01.03.86
Signed	AUGUST 2014
Previous club	ELCHE
Debut	NEWCASTLE UNITED (H) 23.08.14

MIDFIELDER

(On Loan)

Carles Gil

Born	VALENCIA, SPAIN, 22.11.92
Signed	JANUARY 2015
Previous club	VALENCIA
Debut	LIVERPOOL (H) 17.01.15

STRIKER

Ross McCormack

Born	GLASGOW, 18.08.86
Signed	AUGUST 2016
Previous club	FULHAM
Debut	SHEFFIELD WEDNESDAY (A) 07.08.16

MIDFIELDER

Mile Jedinak

Born	SYDNEY, AUSTRALIA, 03.08.84
Signed	AUGUST 2016
Previous club	CRYSTAL PALACE

Mark
Bunn

GOALKEEPER

Born	LONDON, 16.11.84
Signed	JULY 2015
Previous club	NORWICH CITY
Debut	NOTTS COUNTY (H) 25.08.15

Jordan
Amavi

DEFENDER

Born	TOULON, FRANCE, 09.03.94
Signed	JULY 2015
Previous club	NICE
Debut	BOURNEMOUTH (A) 08.08.1

Jordan
Ayew

STRIKER

Born	MARSEILLE, FRANCE, 11.09.91
Signed	JULY 2015
Previous club	LORIENT
Debut	BOURNEMOUTH (A) 08.08.15

Andre
Green

STRIKER

Born	SOLIHULL, ENGLAND, 26.07.98
Signed	ACADEMY GRADUATE
Debut	TOTTENHAM HOTSPUR (H) 13.03.16

Rudy
Gestede

Born	ESSEY-LES-NANCY, FRANCE, 10.10.88
Signed	JULY 2015
Previous club	BLACKBURN ROVERS
Debut	BOURNEMOUTH (A) 08.08.15

(On Loan)

Jordan
Veretout

Born	ANCENCIS, FRANCE, 01.03.93
Signed	JULY 2015
Previous club	NANTES
Debut	BOURNEMOUTH (A) 08.08.15

Albert
Adomah

Born	LONDON, 13.12.87
Signed	AUGUST 2016
Previous club	MIDDLESBROUGH

Rushian
Hepburn-Murphy

Born	BIRMINGHAM, 28.08.98
Signed	ACADEMY GRADUATE
Debut	SUNDERLAND (A) 14.03.15

27

SEASON REVIEW 15-16

AUGUST

Villa couldn't wish for a better start. Summer signing Rudy Gestede makes his entrance as a substitute for another new boy, Jordan Ayew, and in the 72nd minute the Benin international heads home Ashley Westwood's corner to clinch a 1-0 opening–day victory away to Premier League new boys Bournemouth.

Unfortunately, Villa are unable to build on that solid start, slipping 1-0 at home to Manchester United and 2-1 at Crystal Palace before drawing 2-2 against Sunderland. After going behind, Villa storm in front with two goals from Scott Sinclair – one from the penalty spot – only to be pegged back early in the second half.

Sinclair's brace makes it five in two games for the former Manchester City man, who had netted a hat-trick in the 5-3 Capital One Cup victory over Notts County a few days earlier.

SEPTEMBER

Jack Grealish scores his first goal for the first team to open the scoring against Leicester City, and when Carles Gil's screamer makes it 2-0 in the 63rd minute, Villa are on course for three points at the King Power Stadium.

But the visitors are stunned by a late Foxes comeback which leaves them beaten 3-2, and there's another blow when West Brom win at Villa Park the following week.

Rudy Gestede's 62nd-minute header secures victory over our neighbours from across the city in the Capital One Cup, but the striker's two second-half goals are not enough to prevent a 3-2 defeat a Liverpool the following Saturday.

OCTOBER

After setbacks at the hands of Stoke City and Chelsea, Villa seem to be on course for a much-needed win when Jordan Ayew opens the scoring just past the hour mark at home to Swansea City.

But the visitors draw level with a Gyfli Sigurdsson free-kick and three minutes from the end Ayew's brother Andre hits the winner for the Swans. It's our sixth consecutive Premier League defeat, and manager Sherwood is sacked the following day.

Villa also make their exit from the Capital One Cup, Scott Sinclair's last-minute penalty failing to prevent a 2-1 defeat at Southampton.

NOVEMBER

New boss Remi Garde watches from the stand at White Hart Lane as Villa go down 3-1 to Tottenham, our hopes being raised by Ayew's 80th-minute goal and then ended when Harry Kane hits Spurs' third in stoppage time.

There's a big improvement in a goalless draw against Manchester City but it's a very brief honeymoon period for the new manager as Villa slump 4-0 at Everton and then lose 3-2 at home to Watford.

Skipper Micah Richards scores his first Villa goal against the Hornets to make it 1-1 at half-time but the visitors add two more before Jordan Ayew fires home from the edge of the penalty area in the 89th minute.

DECEMBER

Joleon Lescott scores his first goal for the club in a 1-1 draw against Southampton at St Mary's, while Jordan Ayew is on target in successive games against Newcastle United at St James' Park and West Ham at Villa Park on Boxing Day.

While those efforts earn a total of three points, though, Villa suffer 2-0 defeats at the hands of Arsenal and Norwich City to end 2015 at the bottom of the table.

JANUARY →

The new year starts as the old one ends – with a defeat to one of our fellow strugglers. Despite Carles Gil's sensational volley for the equaliser at the Stadium of Light, Villa are beaten 3-1 by Sunderland.

But two consecutive Villa Park fixtures bring much better fortunes. Crystal Palace keeper Wayne Hennessey fumbles Joleon Lescott's header over the line for Villa's first home league success of the campaign and that's followed by a creditable 1-1 draw against Leicester City. Mark Bunn saves a Riyad Mahrez penalty against the Foxes before Rudy Gestede hits a 75th-minute equaliser.

Villa then beat Wycombe Wanderers 2-0 in a third round FA Cup replay, having drawn the original game at Adams Park, before a goalless draw at West Brom makes it five points from three league games.

FEBRUARY

Jordan Ayew is sent off early at Upton Park, leaving the remaining 10 men to fight an uphill battle in a 2-0 defeat by West Ham, but four days later Villa record their third league win of the season.

Remi Garde's side go ahead just before half-time when Joleon Lescott's shot deflects in off Timm Klose, while Gabby Agbonlahor clinches a 2-0 win with a calmly-taken goal on 51 minutes – his first of the campaign.

But the revival is short-lived, Villa crashing 6-0 at home to Liverpool before losing 2-1 to Stoke City at the Britannia Stadium, where Leandro Bacuna scores a79th-minute consolation goal.

MARCH

Rudy Gestede's superb late header from Jordan Veretout's cross is too late to salvage anything in a 3-1 home defeat by Everton, and the agony continues as Villa are outclassed to the tune of 4-0 at Manchester City, all the goals coming in the second half.

Despite an improved display against Tottenham, the visitors maintain their title challenge by scoring just before and just after half-time. And Villa are the better side throughout the first half against Swansea City at the Liberty Stadium, only to lose 1-0.

APRIL

Our worst fears are realised as a 1-0 defeat by Manchester United condemns Villa to relegation in the Championship.

The game at Old Trafford is our ninth consecutive defeat, following back-to-back home setbacks against Chelsea and Bournemouth. Jordan Ayew scores a consolation goal against the Cherries, while Ashley Westwood is on target twice in a subsequent 4-2 defeat by Southampton at Villa Park.

Villa then lead twice against Watford at Vicarage Road, through Ciaran Clark and Jordan Ayew, only to concede two late goals and lose 3-2.

MAY

Villa go into their final home game against Newcastle United knowing that another setback will leave them with an unwanted club record – 12 consecutive defeats.

Thankfully they avoid that particular embarrassment with a battling goalless draw against the Geordies, and the team receive a warm reception from supporters at the end of the match.

Sadly, the players are unable to reproduce such a gritty performance at the Emirates the following weekend, signing off a bitterly disappointing campaign with an emphatic defeat at the hands of Arsenal.

Results and scorers

Date	Fixture	H/A	Score	Scorers
Aug 08	Bournemouth	A	1-0	Gestede
Aug 14	Manchester United	H	0-1	
Aug 22	Crystal Palace	A	1-2	Souare og
Aug 25	Notts County (LC)	H	5-3	Sinclair 3 (1 pen), Adama, Bennett
Aug 29	Sunderland	H	2-2	Sinclair 2 (1 pen)
Sep 13	Leicester City	A	2-3	Grealish, Gil
Sep 19	West Bromwich Albion	H	0-1	
Sep 22	Birmingham City (LC)	H	1-0	Gestede
Sep 26	Liverpool	A	2-3	Gestede 2
Oct 03	Stoke City	H	0-1	
Oct 17	Chelsea	A	0-2	
Oct 24	Swansea City	H	1-2	Ayew
Oct 28	Southampton	A	1-2	Sinclair (pen)
Nov 02	Tottenham Hotspur	A	1-3	Ayew
Nov 08	Manchester City	H	0-0	
Nov 21	Everton	A	0-4	
Nov 28	Watford	H	2-3	Richards, Ayew
Dec 05	Southampton	A	1-1	Lescott
Dec 13	Arsenal	H	0-2	
Dec 19	Newcastle United	A	1-1	Ayew
Dec 26	West Ham United	H	1-1	Ayew
Dec 28	Norwich City	A	0-2	
Jan 02	Sunderland	A	1-3	Gil
Jan 09	Wycombe Wanderers (FAC3)	A	1-1	Richards
Jan 12	Crystal Palace	H	1-0	Hennessey og
Jan 16	Leicester City	H	1-1	Gestede
Jan 19	Wycombe Wanderers (FAC3 replay)	H	2-0	Clark, Gana
Jan 23	West Bromwich Albion	A	0-0	
Jan 30	Manchester City (FAC4)	H	0-4	
Feb 02	West Ham United	A	0-2	
Feb 06	Norwich City	H	2-0	Klose og, Agbonlahor
Feb 14	Liverpool	H	0-6	
Feb 27	Stoke City	A	1-2	Bacuna
Mar 01	Everton	H	1-3	Gestede
Mar 05	Manchester City	A	0-4	
Mar 13	Tottenham Hotspur	H	0-2	
Mar 19	Swansea City	A	0-1	
Apr 02	Chelsea	H	0-4	
Apr 09	Bournemouth	H	1-2	Ayew
Apr 16	Manchester United	A	0-1	
Apr 23	Southampton	H	2-4	Westwood 2
Apr 30	Watford	A	2-3	Clark, Ayew
May 07	Newcastle United	H	0-0	
May 15	Arsenal	A	0-4	

WESTWOOD

Ashley

Stat attack

DEBUTS 2015-2016

JORDAN AMAVI v BOURNEMOUTH (A)

JORDAN AYEW v BOURNEMOUTH (A)

IDRISSA GANA v BOURNEMOUTH (A)

MICAH RICHARDS v BOURNEMOUTH (A)

JORDAN VERETOUT v BOURNEMOUTH (A)

RUDY GESTEDE v BOURNEMOUTH (A)

ADAMA TRAORE v CRYSTAL PALACE (A)

MARK BUNN v NOTTS COUNTY (H)

JOLEON LESCOTT v LEICESTER CITY (A)

JOSE ANGEL CRESPO v STOKE CITY (H)

JORDAN LYDEN v WYCOMBE WANDERERS (A)

ANDRE GREEN v TOTTENHAM HOTSPUR (H)

KEVIN TONER v SOUTHAMPTON (H)

APPEARANCES AND GOALS 2015-16

1 BRAD GUZAN
A 28 league, 4 cup

4 MICAH RICHARDS
A 23(1) league, 4 cup
G 1 league, 1 cup

5 JORES OKORE
A 12 league, 1(1) cup

6 CIARAN CLARK
A 16(2) LEAGUE, 5 cup
G 1 league, 1 cup

7 LEANDRO BACUNA
A 27(4) league, 4 cup
G 1 league

8 IDRISSA GANA
A 35 league, 2(1) cup
G 1 cup

9 SCOTT SINCLAIR
A 19(8) league, 5(1) cup
G 2 league, 4 cup

11 GABBY AGBONLAHOR
A 13(2) league, 2(1) cup
G 1 league

15 ASHLEY WESTWOOD
A 31(1) league, 5 cup
G 2 league

16 JOLEON LESCOTT
A 30 league, 1 cup
G 1 league

17 JORDAN VERETOUT
A 21(4) league, 3(1) cup

18 KIERAN RICHARDSON
A 8(3) league, 4 cup

19 JORDAN AYEW
A 27(3) league, 3(3) cup
G 7 league

20 ADAMA TRAORE
A 0(10) league, 1 cup
G 1 cup

21 ALAN HUTTON
A 26(2) league, 2 cup

23 JORDAN AMAVI
A 9(1) league, 2 cup

24 CARLOS SANCHEZ
A 16(4) league, 3 cup

25 CARLES GIL
A 17(6) league, 3(1) cup
G 2 league

27 LIBOR KOZAK
A 3(1) league, 0(1) cup

28 CHARLES N'ZOGBIA
A 0(2) league

29 RUSHIAN HEPBURN-MURPHY
A 0(1) league

30 ANDRE GREEN
A 0(2) league

31 MARK BUNN
A 10 league, 2 cup

38 JORDAN LYDEN
A 2(2) league, 1(1) cup

39 RUDY GESTEDE
A 14(18) league, 4 cup
G league, 1 cup

40 JACK GREALISH
A 9(7) league, 2(3) cup
G 1 league

43 ALY CISSOKHO
A 18 league, 1 cup

46 KEVIN TONER
A 3(1) league

KEY:
A APPEARANCES
G GOALS
(1) SUBS

Spot the difference

Look at the two pictures carefully.
Can you find five differences between them?

Answers on page 60

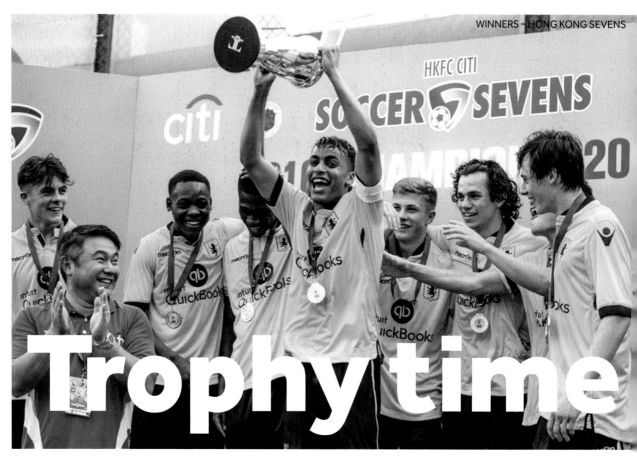

Trophy time

The 2015-16 season wasn't one we will recall with any affection, but it wasn't all doom and gloom at Villa Park.

The club actually picked up three awards, thanks to our younger players, the grounds team and the programme staff.

Villa's youngsters extended their record haul of Hong Kong Soccer Sevens titles by winning the end-of-season event for a record sixth time.

They completed a clean sweep of Group A victories and then progressed to the final, in which they beat West Ham 2-0.

Goals from Harry McKirdy and Rushian Hepburn-Murphy saw off the challenge of the young Hammers to seal a sixth title for Villa, who also triumphed in 2002, 2004, 2007, 2008 and 2010.

And there was a bonus prize for McKirdy, who collected the Golden Boot as the tournament's six-goal leading scorer.

Villa also landed the prestigious Barclays Premier League Grounds Team of the Year award after the playing surface was voted the best in the country.

Grounds manager Paul Mytton proudly holds the trophy, along with his deputy Karl Prescott and staff members Matt Jupp and Ian Hipkiss.

"It's a reward for the enormous amount of hard work, time and dedication from the team," said Mytton.

WINNERS – GROUNDS TEAM

"Just to be in the top five shows we are working at the top of our game. That's a big achievement in itself, and we have done that for the past 10 years. But to actually win the trophy is fantastic."

And the club's programme producers received a special award after the Villa News & Record was voted the best-designed in the Premier League.

WINNERS – VILLA NEWS & RECORD

Villa legend Tony Morley received the trophy from the Northern Programme Club before the final home match of the season, and it then spent 90 minutes on display in the press box as Villa drew 0-0 with Newcastle United.

STILIYAN'S
simply stunning!

Professional footballers are among the fittest people on the planet, but even the most talented players are not always immune from serious illness.

In March 2012, Villa captain Stiliyan Petrov was diagnosed with acute leukaemia and after a year of intensive treatment, he reluctantly conceded that his career was over.

But the Bulgaria international has made remarkable progress since then – to the extent that he resumed training with Villa's first team when the lads reported back ahead of the current season.

None of us could possibly have envisaged such an amazing comeback, and whatever the future may hold Stiliyan has written himself into claret-and-blue folklore.

To be fair, he was a Villa legend even before his illness. Signed from Celtic for £6.5m in 2006, he established himself as an integral member of the team over the following six seasons, playing 218 league and cup games for the club and scoring 12 goals. One of his goals was a sensational lob from the centre circle in a 6-0 win at Derby County.

Petrov made such an impact in midfield that he was appointed captain when Martin Laursen was forced to retire through injury in 2009 – and the following year he led out Villa at Wembley for both the League Cup final against Manchester United and an FA Cup semi-final against Chelsea.

After his leukaemia diagnosis, Villa supporters paid tribute to the man who wore the No. 19 shirt with a minute's applause in the 19th minute of every game.

The lion cubs of Ampertaine...

Going to school can be a lot of fun – particularly when you are learning about Aston Villa!

Just ask the pupils of Ampertaine Primary School. The Northern Ireland youngsters decided to adopt Villa as their favourite English team a few years ago, and their devotion to the club has continued to grow.

The school's curriculum regularly includes lessons and projects based on Villa. And they have even joined the official supporters clubs' network by forming a branch of the Lions Cubs.

So just imagine how delighted both the teachers and the kids were when Villa legend Ian Taylor paid them a visit and took a look at some of their claret-and-blue projects.

Despite being based across the Irish Sea, they also try to visit Villa Park whenever possible and a party of 43 pupils, parents and staff were here for last season's game against Liverpool.

Despite Villa losing 6-0, everyone enjoyed the special Villa Park experience.

"We had a wonderful time," said teacher Ruth Penny. "The hospitality and friendliness of your staff is always superb."

Apart from watching the game, the Ampertaine party had a look around the stadium, with younger fans delighted at the opportunity to go pitch-side.

CHESTER

AVFC

James

STRANGE *but* TRUE

HOLY TRINITY!

We have been proud to call Villa Park our home since 1897 – apart from one season during the Second World War and a couple of weeks early in the Millennium.

In the summer of 2000, Villa competed in the Intertoto Cup for the first time, hoping the inconvenience of starting the season a month early would provide a passage to the UEFA Cup.

There was just one problem. We couldn't play at Villa Park because the new Trinity Road Stand was under construction, so our home ties were staged four miles up the road at The Hawthorns.

Albion's Birmingham Road End was transformed in the Holte End as John Gregory's men beat Marila Pribram 3-1 with goals from Dion Dublin, Ian Taylor and new signing Luc Nilis on Saturday 22nd July, having drawn 0-0 in the Czech Republic in the first leg.

Sadly, there wasn't such a happy outcome when we went back to our temporary home for the second leg against Celta Vigo on Wednesday 2nd August. Villa lost 2-1.

ALL WHITE AT HOME

In a situation few – if any – of us had ever experienced, Villa were forced to switch from the club's traditional colours for the home game against West Ham in April 2009. And the players weren't even able to wear their away kit!

It happened when fellow claret-and-blue outfit West Ham arrived at Villa Park with a pale blue away kit which had been approved by the Premier League.

Unfortunately, referee Rob Styles felt there was still a clash with Villa's sleeves – and the Hammers didn't have any other kit with them, even though it was their responsibility to find an alternative.

At one stage there was even a threat that the match would not go ahead, until Villa boss Martin O'Neill reluctantly agreed that his players would change. Even then, it wasn't possible to wear the away kit because it was blue – so Villa played in white.

It wasn't the first time Villa had been forced to change their kit. In September 1889, after the kick-off at the old Wellington Road ground had already been delayed by 30 minutes because Notts County arrived late, both teams emerged wearing white.

TULIP PICKED TWICE...

Centre-half John Sleeuwenhoek was selected for both Villa and Birmingham City on Friday 3rd November 1967. He was named in the Villa side to face Carlisle United the following day but that afternoon he moved across the city to join Blues for £45,000 – and was picked for their game against Derby County.

Sleeuwenhoek, popularly known as "Tulip" because of his Dutch roots, was actually born in Wednesfield, near Wolverhampton.

THE "HAIRDRYER" TREATMENT!

The Villa Park pitch ranks among the best in the world, but that wasn't always the case. As recently as the early 1990s, there was often very little grass on the playing surface during the winter months.

Even so, the club have always gone to great lengths to avoid postponements. In March 1975, the Second Division match against Southampton was in doubt following five days of rain – so Villa hired a helicopter to dry out the surface.

"It works like a giant hairdryer, sending blasts of air down on to the pitch," explained secretary Alan Bennett.

The idea came from groundsman George Murphy and the helicopter hire cost £250. It was money well spent – Villa won 3-0.

THE LONGEST MATCH

Villa were champions for the fourth time in 1898-99 – despite suffering a 4-1 defeat in a match which took four months to complete!

At the end of November, the kick-off at Sheffield Wednesday was delayed because the referee arrived late, and with less than 11 minutes remaining the game was abandoned because of bad light.

Villa were 3-1 down at the time and the league management committee ruled that the remaining time would have to be played at a later date.

On 13th March, Villa returned to Yorkshire and conceded one more goal in the resumed fixture, although their line-up showed two changes from the original game.

George Johnson replaced Frank Bedingfield, who had scored Villa's goal, while Billy Garratt took over from John Devey.

So it could be argued Johnson and Garratty were Villa's first subs – 66 years before substitutes were introduced!

A LOT OF RIGHT-BACKS!

Johnny Dixon was a proud man when he was presented with the FA Cup by the Queen after Villa beat Manchester United in the 1957 Cup Final.

But Villa's captain had an embarrassing moment before the game while introducing Villa's players to the Duke of Edinburgh.

He was so nervous that he described both Stan Lynn and Peter Aldis as right-backs. The Duke replied: "You seem to have a lot of right-backs in your team!'"

NINE GOALS FOR VILLA DUO

Villa had two players selected by England for the first time in 1882 – and the duo could hardly have made a more explosive start.

Howard Vaughton (pictured) and Arthur Brown were on target a total of nine times in a runaway 13-0 victory over Ireland at the Knock Ground in Belfast, Vaughton scoring five goals while Brown weighed in with four.

Those two began a tradition of Villa players being selected for England. For more than a century, we led the way in providing players for the national side and when Fabian Delph made his international debut in a friendly against Norway in 2014 the figure rose to 72.

Sadly, we lost our place at the top of the England international table when Tottenham Hotspur overtook us the following year.

Getting shirty...

Someone has got in a real mess while printing the names on the back of Villa players' shirts! Can you unravel the correct names by solving these anagrams?

I'M AVA
1

TO HUNT
2

BATHS OIL
3

HE'S A GIRL!
4

TUT OREVE
5

ELK CHIP
6

OH SO SICK!
7

CASH ZEN
8

DEJA INK
9

NOTER
10

Y LEND
11

TWO DO SEW
12

ANSWERS ON PAGE 60

BUNN

Mark

A Villa thriller!

Lee Child is one of the world's most famous thriller writers – and he couldn't have been more thrilled when we asked him to switch fiction for fact.

Lee, whose Jack Reacher novels have sold more than 100 million copies, is now based in New York but has been a Villa fan since he was a boy growing up in Handsworth Wood.

He regularly features the names of Villa players and managers in his books, so when we invited him to be guest editor of the Villa News & Record, he jumped at the opportunity.

"Coming on for the last 20 minutes of a game would have been better!" he said. "But being asked to edit the programme was nearly as good."

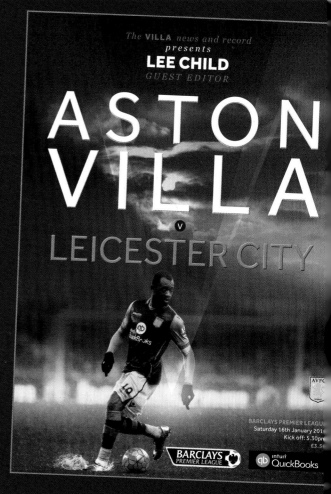

The VILLA news and record presents
LEE CHILD
GUEST EDITOR

ASTON VILLA
v
LEICESTER CITY

BARCLAYS PREMIER LEAGUE
Saturday 16th January 2016
Kick off: 5.30pm
£3.5

BARCLAYS PREMIER LEAGUE

intuit QuickBooks

> ❝ It gave me the chance to remember favourite players and games and to interview Gordon Cowans, my personal all-time best Villan. ❞

Lee was editor for the match against Leicester City last January, liaising via email with our editorial staff at Villa Park. He wrote a welcome message, submitted questions for European Cup hero Gordon Cowans, selected his Star Villa XI, and also provided a few offbeat personal favourites.

CHILD'S CHOICES

MY STAR XI

Guest editor LEE CHILD picks his Villa dream team

We've had some great players over the years. Like Charlie Athersmith, part of the 1896-97 double-winners, who played on the right wing – under an open umbrella if it was raining. And Pongo Waring, who in 1930-31 scored 49 league goals in a 42-match season. As a whole we scored 128 goals that year – three per game. Not bad. But I'm limiting myself to players I actually saw for myself.

GK | NIGEL SPINK (AV)

Nigel Spink had strengths and weaknesses and ups and downs, but in the long run was as good as any keeper Villa ever had. And who can forget the European Cup Final in 1982 – he trotted on after eight minutes as a complete unknown, and 82 ice-cold minutes later he was an enduring legend.

RB | CHRIS PRICE

Not sure why, because there are bigger names, but it's Chris Price. Every game I saw him play was tight, efficient, no fuss, no muss, and I saw him score a great goal, too. And he had a great song – "Chris Price, Chris Price, he's got no hair but we don't care, Chrissie, Chrissie Price."

CB | ALLAN EVANS

Tough choices here, but let's have Allan Evans. Great positioning – a real ball magnet – smooth, unhurried, and reliable. And hard when he needed to be. And he scored some great goals from corners.

CB | PAUL McGRATH

An obvious choice. Slow and crocked most of the time, but still out of this world. I never saw such supernatural anticipation. Time after time I would think, why is he going there? And then the ball would arrive. Sometimes it was McGrath against the opposition for minutes at a time. A genuine superstar.

LB | CHARLIE AITKEN

Charlie made 660 appearances over 17 seasons. To me he was a fixture, like the old A-V floodlights – part of the scenery. He had immaculate timing in the tackle and would have been perfect in today's yellow-card situations. An all-time great – and one of the few historic players who would have looked good today.

MF | DENNIS MORTIMER

Morty, sitting deep. Fantastic gliding runs, accurate passing, great vision – the backbone of our greatest side ever. Also a calm, inspirational captain, and a very nice guy by all accounts.

MF | DAVID PLATT

A great talent, and an even harder worker. For long periods he was our key man – and England's. Countless head-up, chest-out runs from midfield, resulting in countless vital goals. One of the few players you always felt was more likely to score than miss. Priceless.

MF | GORDON COWANS

In my opinion the greatest player we ever had. Sublime passing – he never kicked a ball, but stroked it, caressed it, launched it. He had imagination to spare, and a will to win you could feel at the top of the Holte. Seeing him play was one of the great pleasures of my life.

MF | TONY MORLEY

Wide on the left. Always exciting, always likely to make something happen – and when he was in the zone he was amazing. Just watch the DVD of the 1981-82 European campaign – it was his cup, really, and not just for that vital cross along the six-yard line in the final. Never have good defenders been more embarrassed.

CF | PETER WITHE

Has to be Peter Withe. He gave 110 per cent all the time and chased every lost cause. I saw him score great goals, scruffy goals, lucky goals and accidental goals. I also loved how he loved the fans – no-one treated us better.

CF | BOBBY THOMSON

A purely sentimental choice. Bobby Thomson scored a hat-trick in the first game I ever saw at Villa Park – 21st April 1962, 8-3 against Leicester City. He was big and bustling – not sure how he would make out today, but he was my hero when I was seven.

58 www.avfc.co.uk

PERSONAL...

Lee Child signs off as guest editor with a few personal favourites

BEST SHIRT

Has to be the 1982-83 home shirt - simple, elegant, with the small round "Champions of Europe" badge. It doesn't get better than that. I still have mine.

BEST AWAY GAME NO-ONE ELSE REMEMBERS

November 1982, Stoke 0 Villa 3. A cold day less than a month from Christmas. The heater in my car was bust and I was freezing by the time I got to the Victoria Ground. But two from Gary Shaw plus an own goal gave us a solid win. The place was rocking with 'Jingle Bells, Jingle Bells, jingle all the way, oh what fun it is to see the Villa win away."

BEST FIRST GAME OF THE SEASON

They're all great, really - the joy of having football back, the lush green untouched pitch, the sense of anticipation for what lies ahead. August 1983 against the Baggies was perfect - fantastic, hot sunny weather, a real ding-dong of a game that we won 4-3. I was upstairs in Trinity Road, with a bunch of Baggies fans who had somehow got in there, but we all had fun and got along.

FRIENDLIEST MANAGER

Before I was a writer, I worked for Granada TV in Manchester. In May 1988 we had secured promotion, and I dialled the Villa Park switchboard, and said my name, and said I was calling from Granada, and asked to speak to Graham Taylor. He came on the line (maybe expecting a TV gig?) and I told him it was technically true I was calling from Granada, but only because I was a lifelong fan and wanted to say thanks for a great season and for getting us back to the First Division. He laughed and we talked for an hour. He said I could call back any time, and I did, about six times. Really nice guy.

BEST WEMBLEY WIN

March 1994, the League Cup Final, against Manchester United. They were Alex Ferguson's first great team - Giggs, Cantona, etc - and were overwhelming favourites, but we bossed them from the first whistle and won easily, thanks to Dalian Atkinson and Dean Saunders. A day to remember, for sure.

74 www.avfc.co.uk

It's Villa first, last and always – this club lives on our passion

Remember that line from the first Airplane! movie? Lloyd Bridges says: "Looks like I picked the wrong week to quit drinking." Well, it looks like I picked the wrong season to be guest editor for the News & Record.

Or did I? I'm a Villa supporter, and both those words are crucial. Villa, first, last and always. Supporter, then, now and forever. This is where it counts.

All is not yet lost. Stranger things have happened – including last season, to today's opponents. We have to keep believing. That's what supporters do.

It doesn't matter what the paperwork says at Companies House – this is our club. It belongs to us. It runs on our passion and emotion. If we make it, we can all take the credit.

But if we don't, you can blame me exclusively. On my birthday in 1983 I took my wife to her first game. We sat in the North Stand – and we lost 6-2 to Arsenal. The following year, I took my kid brother to his first game. We stood on the old Holte – and we lost 5-0 to Nottingham Forest. In May last year I flew over from New York for the day and went to Wembley – and you know what happened then. All my fault.

But we always bounced back, better and stronger, and whatever happens this season, we will again – if we keep believing. That's what supporters do. It's time to double and re-double our efforts. We're the claret-and-blue army. When I was a schoolboy we were relegated to the third tier. That was tough. But what did we do? About 15,000 of us went to the first game at Chesterfield. They had never seen anything like it. That's what we do.

If we keep on doing it, all will be well.

ASTON VILLA NEWS & RECORD 2015-16 **05**

These included the friendliest manager (Graham Taylor), the best away game no-one else remembers (Stoke 0 Villa 3 in 1982), the best first game of the season (Villa 4 West Brom 3 in 1983) and the best Wembley win (the 1994 League Cup final).

And in keeping with the occasion, we even switched from our regular front cover to a design based on one of Lee's best-selling novels.

Aiming for the top flight

Villa's priority is to return to the Premier League as soon as possible. Can you help Roberto and the boys? All you need is a dice, two counters and a friend to provide the opposition. First to the top is promoted!

WE'RE UP! ;)	28	27	26	25 ALMOST THERE MOVE ON 3
20	21 STAR FIT AGAIN MOVE ON 4	22 3-MATCH BAN BACK TO START!	23	24 GREAT VOLLEY MOVE ON 3
19 PLAYER INJURED GO BACK 2	18 MATCH POSTPONED MISS A TURN	17	16 VITAL POINTS MOVE ON 2	15
10 BIG WIN MOVE ON 3	11	12 SUSPENSION GO BACK 1	13	14
9 STRIKER LEAVES GO BACK 3	8 PLAYER INJURED GO BACK 3	7 NEW SIGNING MOVE ON 2	6	5
KICK OFF!	1	2 NEW SEASON MOVE ON 2	3	4

AVFC

AMAVI

Jordan

FA CUP

1957

It will be 60 years in May since Villa won the FA Cup for what was then a record seventh time.

Our opponents Manchester United had already clinched the First Division title and were red-hot favourites to become the first team in the 20th century to complete a league and cup double. But Villa had other ideas, recording a 2-1 success, thanks to two second-half goals from Peter McParland.

AVFC

DE LAET

Ritchie

49

THE NUMBERS GAME

16

Rushian Hepburn-Murphy is the youngest player to have represented Villa in the Premier League. He was 16 years and 176 days when he went on as a sub for Christian Benteke in a 4-0 win at Sunderland the season before last.

72

Villa have provided 72 players for the England team. Only Tottenham Hotspur have provided more. The first Villa players to represent their country were Howard Vaughton and Arthur Brown, who scored nine goals between them as England beat Ireland 13-0 in 1882. The last was Fabian Delph, who made his debut against Norway in 2014.

202

Aston Villa v Everton is the most-played fixture in English football – the teams have met 202 times in league games, all of them in the top flight. Hopefully we can look forward to the 203rd meeting in the not-too-distant future!

244

Villa's record scorer is Billy Walker, who netted 244 league and FA Cup goals between his debut in January 1920 and his retirement in November 1933.

660

Left-back Charlie Aitken is the club's record appearance-maker, having played 660 games between 1961 and 1976.

76,588

Villa Park's record attendance is 76,588, for an FA Cup-tie against Derby County in 1946.

1.

2.

3.

Funny faces

Guess whose faces are used to make the funny faces above and below.

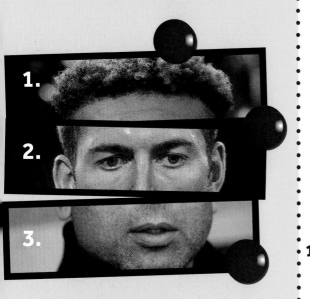

1.

2.

3.

Spot the ball

Can you help Hercules spot the ball in this picture? When you think you know shout 'GOAAAAAAL'

Turn to page 60 to see if you have scored.

A B C D E F G H

1.
2.
3.
4.
5.
6.
7.
8.
9.
10.

STARS OF ⭐ ⭐ ⭐ THE FUTURE

Rushian Hepburn-Murphy

Football clubs often spend millions of pounds on signing big-name players. But clubs can also save a small fortune by developing their own talent – as Villa have proved time and again.

Villa's Academy is regarded as one of the best in the country, has produced some outstanding talent down the years, with youngsters like Lee Hendrie, Darius Vassell, Gareth Barry, Gary Cahill and Gabby Agbonlahor establishing themselves as key members of the first team.

More recently, we have seen Jack Grealish make his breakthrough, while Rushian Hepburn-Murphy became the third-youngest player in the club's history when he made his debut at Sunderland in March 2015 at the age of 16 years and 176 days.

The trend continued last season when three more Academy graduates – Jordan Lyden, Kevin Toner and Andre Green – made their first team debuts. And apart from having a taste of Premier League football, the trio also helped Villa's under-21s to reach the Division Two play-off final.

The team finished fourth in the final table, which earned them a play-off semi-final away to

Kevin Toner

Swansea City. A fine performance saw them emerge 2-1 winners at the Liberty Stadium, thanks to Rory Hale and a Hepburn-Murphy penalty.

Sadly, they were unable to overcome a strong Arsenal side in the final at the Emirates Stadium, losing 3-1 after Hepburn-Murphy had headed them into the lead. But the real success of the under-21s lies with those players who break into Villa's first team.

Andre Green

Jordan Lyden

GESTEDE

Rudy

IT'S SIMPLY SUPER!

JV-Life Super is the best way for young supporters to keep in touch with what's happening to their favourite players.

Four digital editions of the JV-Life magazine email are delivered direct each year to the inbox of every member of Villa's junior club for youngsters aged 14 and under.

And the magazine is now brighter and better than ever. You will find colour photos and interviews with Villa's star players, plus puzzles, comic strips, jokes, competitions and lots more fun-filled pages, all aimed especially at younger supporters.

The magical magazine is just one of the benefits you will receive as a full member of the club. New members receive the following items in their welcome pack:

- A welcome letter from Hercules
- An official JV-Life certificate
- An exclusive JV-Life slap-watch
- A membership card

Members also receive a birthday card and Christmas card, plus invites to exclusive JV-Life parties, where there's often a chance to meet some of Villa's players. Last year we visited Dudley Zoo with Jack Grealish for our Christmas Party.

Your membership card also entitles you to certain discounts around the club including £1 tickets to selected games, 10 per cent discount in the retail store, a free place on our Kickin' Kids Parties plus a free stadium tour. You will also be included in the draw to be a mascot.

All this costs just £19.95 for a whole year!

BENEFITS INCLUDE:

- A welcome letter from Hercules
- An official JV-Life certificate
- An exclusive JV-Life slap-watch
- A membership card
  PLUS SO MUCH MORE!

ONLY
19.95
A YEAR

JV Life Lite

Junior season ticket holders will automatically be JV-Life Lite members, and will continue to receive a host of great benefits including:

- 2 digital magazines
- E-birthday card and E-Christmas card
- £1 tickets to selected games
- 10 per cent discount in retail store
- Free stadium tour place
- Free kids party place
- Chance to be a mascot

JV-Life Lite members can upgrade to JV Life Super for the discounted price of £9.95.

Want to be a mascot?

Being a member of JV Life means you will have the chance to be a match-day mascot, which is an unforgettable experience for any young supporter.

Get a taste for the amazing atmosphere of walking out at Villa Park as a mascot by watching our Mascot Cam from the Villa v West Brom game. Search for 'AVFC mascot cam' on YouTube!

If you are lucky enough to be randomly selected, you will get the chance to display your skills on the pitch before kick-off, sit in the home dug-out, walk out with the players and line-up for the handshakes with the opposition.

You will also receive a souvenir photo of your big day.

FREE MEMBERSHIP FOR JUNIOR SEASON TICKET HOLDERS

For more information, refer to:
avfc.co.uk/fans/junior-villans

Name the managers

1970-1975

1987-1990 &
2002-2003

1998-2002

2003-2006

2006-2010

Can you name these five managers who have been in charge of Villa down the years? To give you a helping hand, we have included the years in which they were the boss.

Let's get quizzical

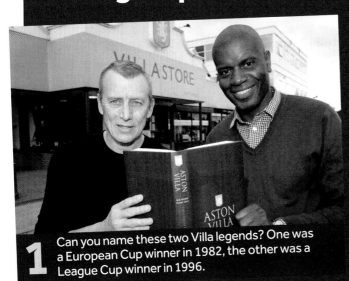

1 Can you name these two Villa legends? One was a European Cup winner in 1982, the other was a League Cup winner in 1996.

2 Which team did Villa beat 2-1 in the semi-final at Wembley to reach the 2015 FA Cup final?

A   Everton
B   Liverpool
C   Chelsea

3 Which new signing was the club's leading scorer with seven Premier League goals last season?

A   Rudy Gestede
B   Scott Sinclair
C   Jordan Ayew

4 What is the name of Villa's cuddly lion mascot?

A   Hercules
B   Hector
C   Horatio

5 How many times have Villa won the FA Cup?

A   Six
B   Seven
C   Eight

ANSWERS ON PAGE 61

McCORMACK

Ross

Can you help Hercules?

Villa Park

START

Can you help me find the way back to Villa Park? I have lost my way.

SOLUTION ON PAGE 61

GREALISH

AVFC

Jack

Answers

Spot the difference page 35

Spot the ball page 51

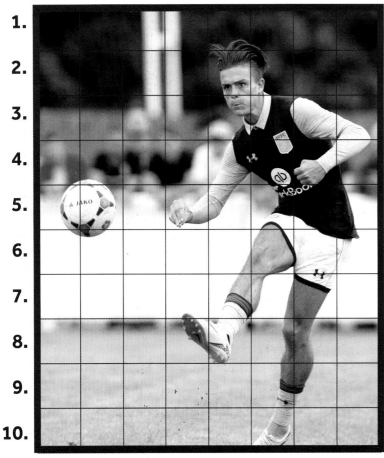

Answer B5

Do you know Ashley Westwood? page 11

1 (b) Crewe Alexandra
2 (a) Swansea City
3 (a) West Brom
4 (b) Southampton
5 (c) Lee Child

Getting shirty page 42

1. AMAVI
2. HUTTON
3. TSHIBOLA
4. GREALISH
5. VERETOUT
6. ELPHICK
7. CISSOKHO
8. SANCHEZ
9. JEDINAK
10. TONER
11. LYDEN
12. WESTWOOD

Funny faces

page 51

First funny face:
1. Jack Grealish
2. Ritchie De Laet
3. Ashley Westwood

Second funny face:
1. Aaron Tshibola
2. Gary Gardner
3. Roberto Di Matteo

Can you help Hercules? page 58

Villa Park

START

International Villans page 15

		H	A	D	J	I		
			B	A	R	O	S	
D	E	L	A	C	R	U	Z	
	Y	O	R	K	E			
	A	N	G	E	L			
	P	E	T	R	O	V		
M	I	L	O	S	E	V	I	C
O	Z	A	L	A	N			
G	I	N	O	L	A			
		G	I	L				
P	O	S	T	M	A			
J	O	H	N	S	E	N		

Where's Hercules?